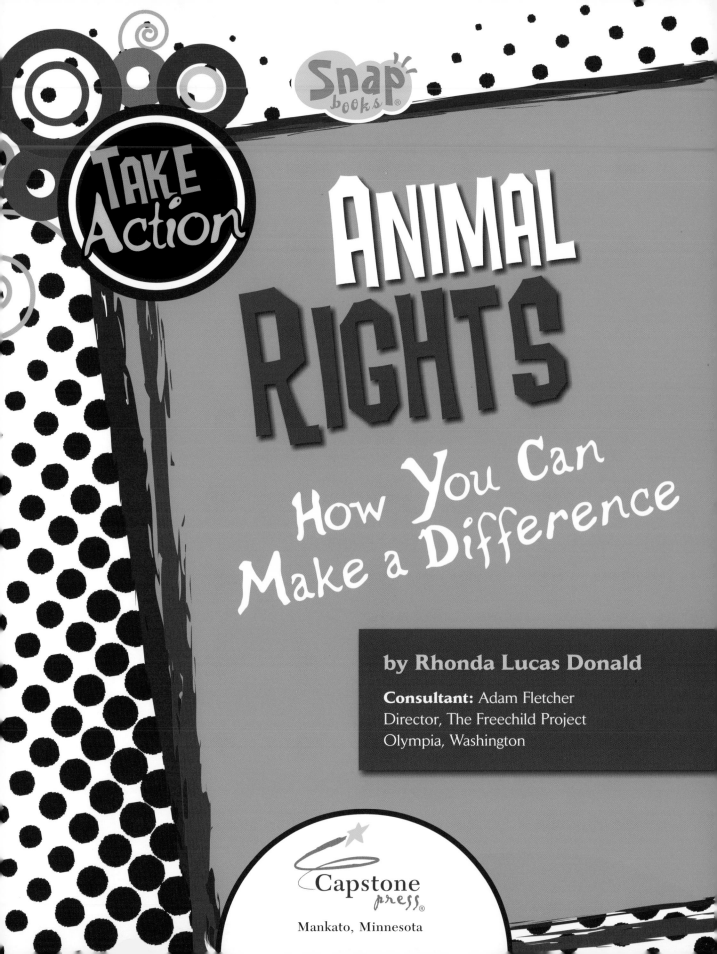

Snap books®

TAKE Action

ANIMAL RIGHTS

How You Can Make a Difference

by **Rhonda Lucas Donald**

Consultant: Adam Fletcher
Director, The Freechild Project
Olympia, Washington

Capstone press®

Mankato, Minnesota

Snap Books are published by Capstone Press,
151 Good Counsel Drive, P.O. Box 669, Mankato, Minnesota 56002.
www.capstonepress.com

Library of Congress Cataloging-in-Publication Data
Donald, Rhonda Lucas, 1962–
    Animal rights : how you can make a difference / by Rhonda Lucas Donald.
    p. cm. — (Snap books. Take Action)
    Includes bibliographical references and index.
    Summary: "Describes what animal rights activism is and serves as a guide explaining how youth can make change in their
world" — Provided by publisher.
    ISBN-13: 978-1-4296-2796-2 (hardcover)
    ISBN-10: 1-4296-2796-4 (hardcover)
    1. Animal rights movement — United States — Juvenile literature. 2. Animal rights activists — United States — Juvenile literature.
3. Animal rights — United States — Juvenile literature. 4. Animal welfare — United States — Juvenile literature. I. Title. II. Series.
HV4708.D66 2009
179'.3 — dc22
                                 2008026943

Editor: Jennifer Besel
Designer: Veronica Bianchini
Photo Researcher: Wanda Winch

Photo Credits: All photos by Capstone Press/Karon Dubke, except:
Alan Mobley, 32 (top)
Courtesy of Adam Fletcher, 32 (bottom)
Courtesy of Amanda MacDonald, 25
Courtesy of Haley Ham, 5, 7 (both)
Courtesy of Long Island Press, 11 (both)
Courtesy of Marcelo Hoynowski, 17
Courtesy of Seema Rupani, 21

Essential content terms are **bold** and are defined at the bottom of the page where they first appear.

1 2 3 4 5 6 14 13 12 11 10 09

Table of Contents

CHAPTER 1

CHANGE FOR THE BITTER

Two of Haley Ham's best friends were dogs, Sam and Jessie. The three of them spent lots of time together. In fact, they were rarely apart. Then one day, Sam got sick. The dog started throwing up and acting strangely. Haley and her mom took Sam to the veterinarian. They learned that the dog had licked up a poisonous chemical. The vet told Haley that her dog would not survive. When Haley returned home, she learned more bad news. Jessie was sick too.

Haley discovered that the chemical the dogs drank was called antifreeze. But this 11-year-old didn't even know what antifreeze was. Haley wondered if there was a way to keep this from happening to other dogs.

Haley decided to take action to prevent other dogs from suffering from antifreeze poisoning like her dog Sam.

The first thing Haley did was learn all she could about antifreeze. Online she learned that antifreeze is used in cars. It keeps water in the engines from freezing, but the chemical can sometimes leak out of cars. The chemical actually smells and tastes sweet.

In her research, Haley also learned that another chemical can be added to antifreeze to make it taste bitter. In fact, adding the bittering chemical is law in some states. Haley wondered why it wasn't law in her state of Tennessee. She believed a new law was needed to save animals from the poison.

First Haley created a 4-H project. Her project informed people about the dangers animals face if they drink antifreeze. Then Haley sent a letter to each state senator in Tennessee. She asked them to help her make a law. Senator Raymond Finney jumped on board. He submitted a bill that would require companies to put the bittering chemical in antifreeze sold in Tennessee. If passed, the bill would become law. But Haley didn't stop there. She set up a Web site and an online **petition**. Haley's petition received almost 2,000 signatures. In February 2008, the Senate voted on the bill. Every senator voted in favor of the bill!

In May, the state House of Representatives also voted to pass the bill. With the governor's signature, the bill became law. It took Haley a lot of time and effort to achieve her goal. But she believed it was important to protect the health of animals. And she's learned a big lesson — one kid can make a huge difference.

petition – a letter signed by many people asking leaders for a change

Haley Ham with Senator Finney

Haley with the governor, signing her bill into law

Powerful You!

Activists are people who see a problem and work to do something about it. Animal rights activists focus their work on helping all kinds of animals. Animal rights activists aren't just adults. Kids are making change everywhere. And so can you!

THINKING UP A CAUSE

BRAINSTORM PROBLEMS

The first step to taking action is easy. It's all about putting a bunch of ideas on paper. Grab a piece of paper and a pencil. Now start thinking of things that bother you or make you concerned. Are you happy with your food choices at school? How do you feel about the way neighbors treat their pets? Do any animal projects in science class worry you? Write down anything you think of. Don't stop to think about how to solve the problems. Just write!

Problems don't have to come from just home or school. Widen your scope to your town, city, or state. Think about what happens to **stray** animals in your town. How do you feel about the animals in cages at the zoo?

The problems you list could even be global. Maybe you've read about whale or seal hunts. Or maybe you've heard about controversial treatment of farm animals. A news story might report on products tested on animals. Ideas can pop up just about anywhere. Whatever you think of, write it down.

Tip If you're having trouble thinking of problems, try this fill-in-the-blank. "It really bothers me when _____." Write down whatever bothers you. Have friends and family fill in the blank too. Their ideas just might spark other ideas.

stray – an animal that is lost or wandering around

BRAINSTORM IDEAS AND PICK A CAUSE

Now it's time to brainstorm ways to solve those problems. You don't need to plan how you'll make the solutions work. Just list some ideas that could solve each problem. Let's say you wrote, "It really bothers me that animals are put to sleep at my town's animal shelter." Your list of solutions might look like this:

- Build a bigger shelter.
- Get more people to adopt homeless animals.
- Offer pet training to people so they won't be upset by their animals and abandon them.

Time to Focus

You have a list of problems. You also have some solutions. Now what? It's time to pick your cause. Look over your list. What cause do you feel strongest about? What would you enjoy working on for hours? Pick the one cause that you really care about.

Sometimes you might want to pick more than one cause. Just pick one to work on now. You don't want to take on more than you can handle. You can come back to the others later. One idea at a time, you can make a difference in the world!

Tim Eisemann was in the sixth grade when his class studied duck eggs and ducklings. After the ducks hatched, Tim got very concerned. He knew the ducks couldn't stay at the school forever. He asked his teacher where the ducks would go. Tim was horrified to learn the ducks would be returned to the farm they came from to be killed. He felt he had to do something. So this 12-year-old hatched a plan of his own.

Tim got on the phone. He called every place he could find that might take the ducks. Place after place refused. Finally he found Karen Davis with United Poultry Concerns. Karen got to work helping Tim save the ducks. One of Karen's contacts sent out an emergency e-mail alert. Within minutes of the e-mail, Tim was talking to people from Angel's Gate. This center cares for animals with special needs. Angel's Gate agreed to take the ducks. The ducklings would be safe and cared for the rest of their lives.

Tim and Karen also told the media about the problem. People began questioning the school's hatching program. Because of Tim's work, the ducks were saved, and the school ended its hatching experiments.

Tim Eisemann

GETTING ALL THE FACTS

STEP 3: RESEARCH, RESEARCH, RESEARCH

Before dashing in to save the animals, you've got to know your topic. People are bound to ask you questions. You don't want to say something that isn't correct. Doing so might harm your cause. You need to become an expert on your issue. And that means research.

Thousands of Opinions

When you research, remember that no issue is one-sided. You will definitely find people who disagree with your ideas. Everyone is allowed to have opinions. And opinions aren't right or wrong.

It's always a good idea to learn about other ideas. If you know what others believe, you'll be able to make a stronger case for your change. And once in a while, someone's opinion could change your mind. That's all right too. Step 3 is about gathering every bit of information you can. You will probably learn things you didn't know before.

To the Library

Where can you get books, magazines, newspapers, and DVDs? If you said the library, you're right. The library is a great place to start your research. Librarians can help you find all kinds of resources about your topic. Just ask them.

Then dig in. Read, watch, or listen to every reliable piece of information you can find. Take notes on the information you gather. And don't forget to write down where you found your facts. You'll be amazed at what you learn.

To the Web

Another great place to find information is online. Watch videos of animal rights protests. Listen to podcasts featuring animal experts. Read about the history of your issue or about the current laws being passed.

You'll also find a lot of networking sites. These sites connect people with similar views. You could chat with other activists about what they are doing. Remember to be careful online, though. Don't give out personal information to people you don't know.

To the People

People will also be some of your best resources. Experts have done a lot of research themselves. If you can, contact these experts. You might be surprised by the information they will share with you. A diet specialist can help you find facts about eating **vegetarian**. Someone with your local humane society can help you learn about pet issues. A nature center is a good place to learn about wildlife. Interview experts, and ask them your questions. Share your ideas with them, and listen to their opinions too.

As you did your researching, you probably learned of organizations working on a cause like yours. Contact leaders in animal rights organizations as well. You should be able to find contact information on their Web sites. Learn about the actions they are taking. Talk to them about your ideas. They might have some helpful resources for you.

vegetarian – eating only plants and plant products and sometimes eggs or dairy products

Question It

As you're digging through information, you might find some facts that support different points of view. Say you are researching the treatment of farm animals. An animal rights group might say cattle suffer when killed for meat. Meat producers might point out that they obey laws about animal treatment. Both groups want to sway your opinion in their favor. It's important to ask questions about the information you're getting. Here are some questions to ask.

Is the information from a trusted **source**? Universities and research centers are often good sources. Animal protection groups might also have good information for you. Just remember that people can post anything online. Always double check your facts.

Is the information based on stereotypes? No two people are exactly alike. If you hear someone say, "Rich people have animals killed so they can wear fur," question it. Broad statements probably aren't entirely true.

Does the information seem incomplete? People might leave out facts that hurt their case. Digging into lots of sources will help you find all the facts. A good piece of information will explain all sides of a topic.

> ## Tip
> Which Web sites can you trust? Check the address for a clue. Information from government agencies is usually carefully researched. Their sites end in .gov. Universities are also good sources. Their addresses end in .edu.

source — someone or something that provides information

Marcelo Hoynowski has never been to Canada. He's never seen a harp seal in person. But that hasn't stopped this 12-year-old from doing all he can to stop Canadian harp seal hunting.

Marcelo read an article that said each year people legally hunt harp seals in Canada for their fur. The hunters use clubs or ice picks to kill the seals. Even though Marcelo lives in New Jersey, not Canada, he wanted to stop the hunts.

Marcelo decided that the best way to stop the hunts was to tell people about them. He got to work doing research. He read information from the National Geographic Society, the Canada Department of Fisheries and Oceans, and many other sources.

With the information he found, Marcelo created a Web site of his own. His site is full of facts about seals and the hunts. It has information about what people can do to help. The site has had as many as 30,000 visitors in one month. Marcelo is spreading his message, one click at a time.

Marcelo Hoynowski

MAPPING OUT YOUR ACTION

STEP 4: SET A GOAL AND MAKE A PLAN

You've brainstormed ideas and done your homework. You're ready to set a goal. The more specific your goal, the more likely you are to succeed. If your goal is to protect all animals, that's too big. If your goal is to raise $50,000 to build an animal shelter, you will know exactly what you're aiming for.

A clear goal will also help you with the rest of step 4. This step is all about planning what you're going to do. Figure out what you'll need, who to talk to, and how long it will take. As you're planning, don't be afraid to ask for help. Others might have new ideas.

Here are some good questions to ask yourself as you're making your plan:

- Who are the people you'll need to contact for help? In your research, you learned about people and groups who could help you. Sometimes a national group can put you in touch with activists in your area. You'll also need to meet or talk to local people who make the decisions.
- What are you doing? Will you join a club to try to get vegetarian food at school? Will you talk to politicians about a law to stop animal abuse?
- When are you going to do this, and how long will it take? Consider setting a time frame to have each part of your plan finished. Then you'll be able to keep your work on track.
- Where are you going to do this? Before doing anything, you need permission from those involved. At school, you should check with your club adviser or principal. If you plan a public event, you'll need permission from the school, town, county, or business.
- Why are you taking this course of action over another? Why do you think this is the best way to achieve your goal?
- How? Plan your action step-by-step. Figure out the items you need or the advertising you'll do. How many volunteers will you need?

Use Your Talents

As you make a plan, think about things you do really well. Put your talents to use. If you're great on the computer, plan to make a Web site. Maybe baking is your skill. A booth full of your goodies could be a great fund-raiser. No matter what you're good at, find a way to use your talents to help you reach your goal.

Cause and Effect

Before you get out there and take action, it's a good idea to think about how your plan will affect you or others. If you're planning to **picket** a fast food restaurant, you might bother customers. If you want to boycott school lunch, you could have the principal mad at you. Some risks are okay to take. As you learned earlier, not everyone will agree with you. But if your actions are too risky, they could affect people in a negative way. Not only could people get hurt, but you could lose support for your cause. Think your plan through. Consider the risks you'll be taking. If you're not sure about your ideas, talk with other people. They might be able to help you figure out if your actions are worth the risk.

picket — to stand outside a place to spread your message

Action Spotlight

Seema Rupani became a vegetarian because she didn't like the idea of killing animals for food. But her school didn't offer vegetarian lunch options. In her junior year of high school, Seema started a club called the Youth Humane Society (YHS). The club's goal was to get vegetarian options on the lunch menu.

Seema and other YHS members collected more than 1,000 signatures from students asking for vegetarian choices. Then Seema took the petitions to the principal and the food services director. She explained the reasons behind the club's request. The school agreed to offer vegetarian options on a trial basis. The day the veggie options were offered, the food sold out in five minutes. The more foods they offered, the more they sold. Eventually vegetarian options were added to the school menu permanently.

Seema Rupani (second from right)

CHAPTER 5

TAKE ACTION!

STEP 5: PUT YOUR PLAN INTO ACTION

Planning a big project is exciting. Seeing it through is even more exciting. And it's also hard work. But if you really care about your cause, all that work will be worth it.

As you get rolling on your plan, you'll want to find others who will help. You don't have to do everything by yourself. Start by telling your friends and family members about your idea. You could send out e-mails, make phone calls, or talk to them in person. Spread your excitement. But don't worry if some don't agree to help. Even some people you are close to might disagree with your opinion. That's okay. Be respectful, but keep working toward your goal.

Once you've talked to people you know, reach out to people you don't know. Talk with community leaders or teachers. Give presentations to local clubs. Step 5 is about getting out there and spreading your message.

When you have some people willing to help, assign each person a job. If your friend is a great speaker, have him give more presentations. If your uncle owns a sign shop, have him make some banners. Get your group out there. Whatever you do, you're taking action!

Tip Consider building your events around special days. Some examples are World Farm Animals Day, Great American Meatout, and Animal Shelter Appreciation Week. Sponsors of these national events offer resources you can use.

Get the Word Out

You might not actually have to talk to spread your message. You can create posters, flyers, or displays. Libraries are great places to put up displays that reach lots of people. How about writing an article for your school newsletter? You can post on a blog. T-shirts are another great way to get attention. A cool design or catchy phrase will get people interested. When they ask you about your shirt, tell them what you're doing. You just might get someone else to join your cause.

The media is a powerful tool for getting attention. Contact TV and radio stations and newspapers. Let them know what you're doing. You just might see your picture and your message plastered on the front page of the paper.

Cool, Calm, and Collected

When you're out there making change, you'll probably run across people who disagree with you. Some people are very passionate about their beliefs. They aren't afraid to tell you what they think. Be polite when others talk to you about different ideas. You don't have to agree with them. But you'll always gain more support for your cause if you are respectful.

When Amanda MacDonald was 13, she learned about the Committee to Protect Dogs. The group believed that greyhound racing was cruel to the dogs. The group was trying to stop greyhound racing in Massachusetts. Because she loved dogs, Amanda decided to help.

People in Massachusetts must vote to ban racing. But the issue couldn't be put on the ballot without enough signatures on a petition. Amanda decided to help by collecting 400 signatures. She began bringing her petition everywhere. Amanda got people to sign at tennis practice, at school, and even at the dentist's office. She went door-to-door talking to people. Then Amanda got permission from her town to hold a rally. At the rally, she told people about her cause and gathered more support. One of her state senators even came to the rally and signed Amanda's petition. With her help, the committee got enough signatures. Massachusetts voters get to decide if greyhound racing should continue in their state.

Amanda MacDonald (right)

You Can Make a Difference

A lot of time and energy goes into making change happen. But if you don't do it, who will? Once in a while, you might be disappointed. Don't let disappointment stop you. Changing people's minds is not easy. Getting people to change their behavior can be even tougher. But if you present your ideas well and in a positive way, you'll make an impression. If you rescued even one animal from a shelter, you've made change. If one store stopped selling products made from fur, you've made a difference.

And your action doesn't have to stop when your plan is done. Go back to your list of problems and solutions. Pick a new cause, and build a new plan. Or you can keep working on the same cause with a new plan. Whatever you do, you'll be changing your world. Get out there and take action!

RESOURCES

There are hundreds of resources that can help you be an animal rights activist. Below is a short list to help you get started in your research. But don't stop with this list. Find your own resources that will help you reach your goal.

American Society for the Prevention of Cruelty to Animals

The American Society for the Prevention of Cruelty to Animals has been working to fight animal cruelty since 1866. Located in New York City, ASPCA hosts an educational Web site and runs an animal shelter and veterinary hospital. Its humane law enforcement officers fight crimes against animals in New York.

Animal Concerns

Animal Concerns is an Internet-based group that provides information on animal rights and animal welfare resources. Information is organized by topic. There are sections devoted to action, education, news, and publications.

The Animals Voice

The Animals Voice is a non-profit animal rights organization that works to inform people about animal rights issues. The organization's Web site offers articles, images, fact sheets, and links to thousands of activist and animal rights groups.

The Freechild Project

The Freechild Project is a program that provides tools, training, and advice to youth activists. The project's Web site offers information on a variety of issues and actions. There are many free resources and ideas for youth to use to work toward change in their worlds.

Humane Society of the United States

Based in Washington, D.C., the Humane Society of the United States is the nation's largest animal protection organization. HSUS members work to educate people about animal issues. They also investigate animal cruelty and work with corporations for animal-friendly policies.

People for the Ethical Treatment of Animals

People for the Ethical Treatment of Animals is the largest animal rights group in the world with nearly 2 million supporters. PETA members focus their efforts on stopping and preventing cruelty to animals.

Vegetarian Resource Group

Vegetarian Resource Group educates the public about vegetarianism. They inform people about how the lifestyle relates to health, ecology, and world hunger. VRG publishes the *Vegetarian Journal* and offers recipes and information on its Web site.

WireTap Magazine

WireTap is an online magazine for young people who want to create social change. The focus is on news and culture. Topics covered include politics, racial justice, war and peace, education, and the environment.

Glossary

brainstorm (BRAYN-storm) – to think of many ideas without judging them as good or bad

cause (KAWZ) – an aim or principle for which people believe in and work

controversial (kon-truh-VUR-shuhl) – causing a lot of argument

petition (puh-TISH-uhn) – a letter signed by many people asking leaders for a change

picket (PIK-it) – to stand outside a place to spread your message

source (SORSS) – someone or something that provides information

stereotype (STER-ee-oh-tipe) – an overly simple opinion of a person, group, or thing

stray (STRAY) – an animal that is lost or wandering around

sway (SWAY) – to change or influence how someone thinks or acts

vegetarian (vej-uh-TAIR-ee-uhn) – eating only plants or plant products and sometimes eggs or dairy products

Read More

Botzakis, Stergios. *What's Your Source?: Questioning the News.* Media Literacy. Mankato, Minn.: Capstone Press, 2009.

Lewis, Barbara A. *The Teen Guide to Global Action: How to Connect with Others (Near and Far) to Create Social Change.* Minneapolis: Free Spirit, 2008.

Newkirk, Ingrid. *50 Awesome Ways Kids Can Help Animals: Fun and Easy Ways to Be a Kind Kid.* Boston: Warner Books, 2006.

Internet Sites

FactHound offers a safe, fun way to find educator-approved Internet sites related to this book.

Here's what you do:

1. Visit *www.facthound.com*

2. Choose your grade level.

3. Begin your search.

This book's ID number is 9781429627962.

FactHound will fetch the best sites for you!

Index

Meet the Author

Rhonda Lucas Donald became a vegetarian in her 20s and does her part to promote animal protection by writing for groups that work to help animals. She also volunteers at her local humane society.

Among Rhonda's credits are work for Discovery Channel, Humane Society of the United States, National Geographic Society, National Wildlife Federation, and the Smithsonian Institution.

Meet the Consultant

Adam Fletcher is a private consultant who has worked with thousands of youth and adults, teaching them how to share their energy and wisdom with each other. He started The Freechild Project to share resources with kids on how to change the world. He also created SoundOut to teach people in schools how to listen to student voice.